*W*idows' Depressive Episodes

Shirley D. Frigillano, PhD

WIDOWS' DEPRESSIVE EPISODES
SHIRLEY D. FRIGILLANO
March 2022
Philippines

Edited by: Adrian Fisga Luague
Cover design and Interrior layout by: Romeo C. Morales Jr.

Copyright © 2022 Shirley D. Frigillano

ISBN-13: 979-8440283190

Published by:
ME Publications
Phase 2, Blk. 57, Lot 28
Celine Homes Subdivision
Bacolod City, 6100 Philippines

DEDICATION

This work is dedicated to all newly widowed people, particularly the informants I personally interviewed, as well as three lovely people in my life: my husband, William, and my sons, Eros Gwen and Mishael Shem, who inspire me to write. All honor and glory be to God Almighty, to Whom I owe all wisdom and strength in completing this literary work.

PREFACE

One painful truth about life is its finality or the inevitable moment when one partner has passed away, and the other is left alone. Death, thus, is an unexpected ending of a relatively happy, intimate bond between a husband and wife. In the face of such loss, it seems impossible that life can continue and have any meaning at all. The grieving partner begins living on a solitary journey of widowhood.

Considered a distressing reality, widowhood is a situation that seriously affects the psychological well-being of the widowed. It is a pathetic condition for widows who have to live alone and survive its ill effects, especially in its early years. If the attachment is deep and strong, it may seem difficult to accept the painful reality and let go of the deceased partner.

This book delves into the lives of eight bereaved women who suffered from depression after the deaths of their husbands. Their stories will provide readers, particularly those who have recently been bereaved, with insights into the grief process and coping strategies when their spouses die.

Shirley D. Frigillano, PhD
Author

FOREWORD

Throughout time and history, there is one thing that stands out above all the other human natures: the bond of relationship and love. It is an unfathomable wonder of human behavior when two people in love let go of their comfort and build their own family in the sacred bond of marriage. Then, through ups and downs, two hearts grow stronger together, drifting towards mutual dependence on most aspects of their being.

Now, the distressing truth of human nature comes into the scene – a time will come when one will depart from this life, scarring the bonds of the heart. The pain and anxiety of this mortal separation are a lethal blow to the surviving partner. How will they live each day without their better half? How will they let go of the pain and anxiety that grief has brought? How will they go on with this earthly voyage for the missions left for them to sustain?

Dr. Shirley D. Frigillano's *Widows' Depressive Episodes* takes us to eight real-life stories and first-hand experiences of strong women, eight widows, who have been through the bitter-sweet taste and skirmishes of married life.

Delve into each page, and discover the stories of Bev, Meg, Nica, Ella, Belen, Rosa, Angel, and Maria, as they unfold and share the taste of love, struggles, grief, and moving forward with lessons! As a whole, Widows' Depressive Episodes is a must-have book to read and add to your library collections!

Kudos to Dr. Shirley D. Frigillano, for shaping this material of great significance towards the world's understanding of life within and beyond marriage. *Padayon!*

Adrian Fisga Luague, CBA
NBDB Certified Author and Editor
Executive Vice President and Editor in Chief, ME Publications
Founder, Peace and Love Inkers Society

TABLE OF CONTENTS

Widows' Depressive Episodes

Death is inevitable. It is an appointment that can never be postponed or canceled. It comes to anybody, at any age, at any time. A person may anticipate death and once it happened, it leaves sorrow and pain to the loved ones. It is a painful reality that is really hard to accept, the finiteness of humanity.

The loss of a loved one, especially of a spouse, is a devastating event. On the part of the grieving partner, it is the most unwanted experience especially if the husband and wife are deeply attached to each other.

The following are the stories of the eight selected newly widowed who experienced depressive episodes over the loss of their husbands.

Story 1: Bev's Trails and Trials

Bev was a plain housewife with five children. Her husband was a tricycle driver. Despite their meager income, the couple was still able to send their children to school. Their other children, being achievers, were able to continue their studies through scholarships extended by the government. They stayed in a simple house, surrounded by close relatives.

Bev and her husband were both residents of the same place. Bev shared that her husband served as a bridge for a friend who was, actually, the one courting her.

The bridge who had a secret admiration for her turned out to be the one who captured Bev's heart. So, they ended up with each other. Bev described her husband as handsome and loving. Most of all, he was a responsible father to their children.

Being hardworking, he won as a barangay councilor and served for 11 years before he got sick. The family simply lived on his income from driving, augmented by an honorarium he received as barangay councilor. Bev, being contented with a simple life, was happy with the man he married. However, life has twists and turns, Bev's fate suddenly changed when her husband got sick.

Her loyalty as wife and mother was tested in the midst of the difficulty of taking care of a sick husband until the finality of death came.

Death: A Melting Candlestick

Bev's husband was driving a tricycle when he felt something unusual in his body. It was the first sudden attack that made her husband go home early that day, uneasy and melting like a candle. According to Bev, because her husband looked pale, she rushed him to a doctor for a check-up. His blood pressure shot up. He was immediately given medication which temporarily alleviated the situation. Bev, seeing no change in her husband's physical condition and not satisfied with the findings of the first doctor, took him to another physician for a second opinion. He was again given medication but after a year, there was no improvement in his physical condition. Bev's husband stopped driving and was confined at home because his health was deteriorating. The family decided to have him admitted to the hospital for proper diagnosis and care. The family of Bev's husband sold a piece of land just to provide for this need. He underwent ECG and it was found out that Bev's husband had a heart enlargement.

After determining the ailment and with proper medicine, he got well. He was back to work as a barangay official. Bev's husband, being a barangay official, was hardworking. He was always busy attending to the needs of the barangay. He dared to lift heavy things; he fixed electrical lines and did other tasks in the barangay. Believing he was well, he was back to the usual routine, until one day, he got ill again.

He was brought back to the doctor again and was given the needed care.Upfront, the doctor told Bev that her husband would only be staying for four years.

Only medicine sustained his life.

Bev felt sad and desperate hearing that her husband's death was already predetermined. Feeling ill and weak, Bev's husband just stayed at home to rest. He would be seen sitting on the balcony of their house, being served by Bev. Four years, appointed by the heart specialist passed by, but Bev's husband was still alive. Bev was consoled by seeing her husband survive the four years set by the doctor. Normally, her husband would just be at home while Bev kept doing her daily tasks. At that time, the eldest son was already supporting the needs of the family and medicine maintenance. The family of Bev's husband somehow shared their support in any way they could. Other children in the family were sent to school, others were government scholars, so Bev would only focus on the medicine of her husband. Life was also tough for the family, yet, Bev patiently bears the situation. Life went on for Bev as if everything was normal.

Days passed; Bev observed something strange about her husband. Bev noticed that her husband would say something unusual. He would talk about family life. He would stare around the house as if checking every corner. One day, he requested Bev to cook the food he liked to eat. Bev did cook what he liked. That was served as his meal at breakfast.

Widows' Depressive Episodes

In the usual setting, he would sit outside and talk with relatives and neighbors passing by. The house of Bev was just beside her husband's family. After an hour, he went inside the room and talked to his children. At that moment, Bev was in her mother's mini-store in the street for a chat.

Later, her daughter came running, saying that her father was not responding. He was lying in bed with his eyes closed and somewhat breathless. The daughter shared that while they were having a talk, the father said that he wanted to sleep. Knowing this, Bev hurriedly ran back to the house with thoughts of doubt and fear about her husband, *Diyos ko, gakadlaw pa tu kaina, wara run, daw indi mapatihan*; (Oh God, he was still smiling before I left. I could hardly believe it.)

Bev's initial actuation was to hurry back to the house, *Nagdalagan ako eh, wara pa ko kaintiyende, wara ko ti bra mong, wara ko ti tsinelas, hingagaw ko bay, wara ko ti bra syempre ja ko sa blay eh. Primero wara ko kahibi mong, wara ko kahibi, urihi di lang nga man-an ko nga patay run*; (I hurriedly ran home although things were not clear. I wore no slippers and rushed him to the clinic hoping he would be revived. I did not cry until I knew he was dead.) These were Bev's feelings and actuations at that moment. She immediately rushed him to the municipal emergency clinic hoping he would still recover. That moment Bev saw that her husband's pants were wet.

Although doubt assailed her, she recalled what the doctor had said before while he was still in the hospital; yet, Bev even at the last moment, still hoped for a miracle that he could still survive.

Days of Torment

The following days that followed were filled with inexplicable sadness and sorrow for Bev. She found herself quiet most of the time. She did not mind other people around. It took one week for Bev to feel the severe pain of the loss of her husband. *Daw mapatay ako, daw masunod ako kana mong; katu nga mga one week wara ako ti ginainom nga bulong, gapungko ako daw indi ko kaginhawa;* (I felt like I wanted to die, too. I felt I was short of breath that moment.) Bev was given medicine to calm down until the burial.

It took three months for Bev to recover from the loss. She would utter statements directed to her husband as if he were present. She would ask for help regarding the needs of the children, *Buligi lang ako kay tungod duro bata ta; palinunga lang ako bala, taw-i lang ako ti mayad nga lawas, makagiya pa ako sa mga kabataan natun;* (Just help me with our children. Give me peace; give me good health to guide our six children).

Also, Bev was reminded of her husband's presence every time it was their barangay fiesta. She recalled how happy they were together dancing and singing.

Bev felt saddened recalling how she took care of her husband's needs--while taking a bath, giving him the towel, soap, serving him his food, water, and medicine. Although it was difficult, she was not tired of serving him while he was sick.

When asked about her unusual actuations about the death, she shared that, *Nag-abat ako sa centro, samtang gapanaw ako, tu ko nagpautwas, ridto ko nagsinggit, wara ko mayha, mu tu nahaw-asan ako, tu ko naghibi todo sa central, duro mga maestro; Bisan duro tawo gali wara kaw mayha basta nabatyag mo, gapanaw ko tingala mga tawo todo akun ngawngaw;* (When I went to see his twin sister who was a teacher, I was screaming in tears while walking. When I reached school, there, I could not hold what was inside me, the pain that I felt; I burst into deep tears before other teachers. I didn't care at all what they would think. I expressed my grief that way at that very moment).

Upon the death of her husband, Bev was worried and anxious about many things. She was thinking about how she would be able to surpass all the problems without her husband- having six children, fear and anxiety about their future beset her, how she could feed and send them to school. Bev lost weight with the loss of her partner.

Bev had no plan of marrying again. At 45, she looked pretty and capable of falling in love again. To her, she would just devote her time to her children. She had buried her love for her

husband. She had best loved him. There were temptations but her husband was always in her mind. She would never find another love as she shared.

Bev and her husband had no other desire than to see their children succeed in life. Education was their priority despite the hardships of life. The death of her husband was the most devastating loss to Bev and with it, she also lost the love of a husband she used to feel. The absence of her husband left an empty feeling and insecurity, especially since everything was managed by her husband -- the finances of the family. As a non-working wife, it was too difficult for Bev. She was just thankful that her eldest child had a job and somehow had helped in any way. The death of Bev's husband brought about change in her. The manner of treating her children was different. She used to nag her children from time to time. But since her husband died, she became less vocal with the loss of her husband. There would no longer be a father to remind the children of the do's and the don'ts at home in just a few words.

The absence of her husband left Bev with sad and happy memories -- the time when her husband would bring home some food for them to eat together; when a misunderstanding arose, her husband would start teasing her until she would start laughing. Bev admitted she was the kind of person who easily bears grudges. If conflicts arose between them, usually, Bev wanted her husband to give up until they came terms again. This was what she missed whenever misunderstandings among her children intervened.

Bev patiently took care of her sick husband since he stopped driving a tricycle.

Struggling Against All Odds

In order to alleviate the pain, Bev spent more time working hard for her family. She exerted more effort in the household chores. She had good sleep but there were times when Bev would wake up in the middle of the night and she would be full of her husband's thoughts and memories. Somehow, it helped her momentarily to fill in her deep longing for her husband.

Bev also gained strength from the eldest son who kept calling and comforting her every day, weeks after the burial, *Ang subang ko adlaw-adlaw na gid ko ginatawgan, ginaestorya na ko bala, ginalaygayan na ako*; (I found comfort in my eldest son who keeps calling me up). She was also comforted by the presence of her other children near her. With more children around, Bev somehow found solace especially if they went working altogether or watching television. Sometimes, Bev joined with other people in the barrio, talking and sharing thoughts with them. She also took time visiting friends and spent time with them to forget the grief, *Galagaw ako, gapabanwa ako, makigkita ako sa mga miga ko* (I spent time talking with some friends who are living in town).

She tried to get comfort through their advice and encouragement to move on and devote time to her children. She also gained comfort from other widows who had the same loss. Seeing them survive the grief gave her strength and encouragement to face the life of a single parent. Sometimes, she felt sad thinking her husband died without experiencing the convenience of life as the fruit of the children's effort and success. Bev admitted that it was hard for her to accept the death of her husband but reminiscing how her husband battled with the illness made her accept it with all her heart. She had accepted that her husband's life was already determined by the ailment from which he suffered. She could not afford to see him in an incapacitated situation and thinking how she could provide his medicine to sustain his life.

Her husband had finally reached his appointment of death. For Bev, seeing her batch mates and relatives around made her lonely, with a deep longing for her husband's presence. She felt better if she could visit friends who gave her comfort.

Story 2: Meg's Grief and Afflictions

Meg was born to a poor family. Her father was a hardworking carpenter while her mother was a good cook. Although their life was described to be below the poverty line, Meg, being the youngest among the five children, did not experience hardship. She was well taken care of by a nanny. At that time, her mother was working as a cook in a restaurant in Manila. Somehow, all the children in the family were sent to school, with Meg reaching her first year in college. She took an Information Technology course; however, she was forced to stop school because her father got injured in carpentry work. Her mother transferred to a nearby eatery or a *Talabahan* at Meg's place. This was the source of living for the family. Meg helped serve as a waitress in that eatery in order to augment the family's income. It was in this *Talabahan* that she met a member of the Philippine Army, who eventually became her life partner.

Two Hearts Become One

Love at first sight struck the army man upon seeing Meg one day when he and his teammates of soldiers dropped by the *Talabahan* to eat. The first casual encounter was followed by frequent rendezvous after getting Meg's cell phone number. Looking pretty and young at 19, Meg might have left a stunning aura to the soldier; and in smart army uniform, Meg might have easily and quickly felt the fast heartbeat for him. Eventually, a romantic relationship started.

Meg admitted she was easily turned on with the man with not many vices like smoking, drinking, and womanizing. According to Meg, after a number of relationships with different types of fellows – student, seaman, doctor, engineer, etc. - she wanted to be linked with an army man. To her, she revealed, the man was her 31st relationship while to him, Meg was the second girl he seriously had a relationship with. The courtship did not last long, the army man won Meg's heart, and after four months, they had a civil marriage.

Finding the man lovable and responsible, Meg agreed to be married to him with the consent of her parents. She got married at 19. They lived together and bore two children, ages six and three at the time her husband died. The eldest child was first sent to a private school but with the death of her husband, she was transferred to a public school. The marriage lasted only six years and 11 months when the husband got killed.

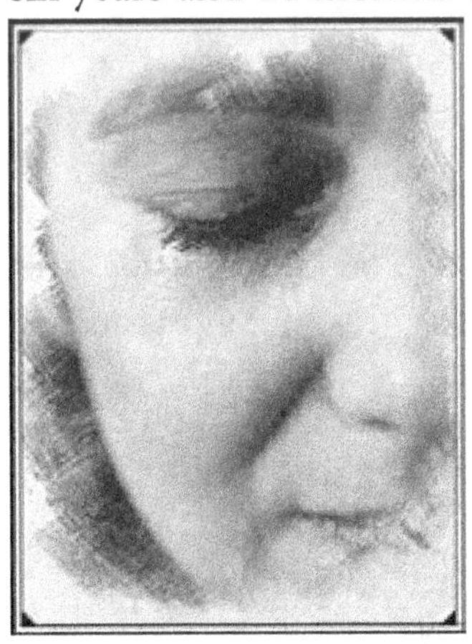

Grief: The Hardest Thing

The terrifying death of Meg's husband took its toll on her happy married life. She was at home waiting for supper when someone came and informed her that her husband met an accident, *Daw napusdakan ako ka langit;* (It seemed like heaven had fallen apart.) This was what Meg shared when she heard the unexpected bad news about the brutal killing of her husband who, at that time, was assigned in Antique. The six years of marriage between Meg and her husband were wrecked by his horrible death and waves of sadness overwhelmed her day and night.

Seeing the lifeless body of her husband in a funeral parlor almost broke her heart. She wanted to believe it was a big mistake to inform her that her husband had an accident and did not survive. Seeing the husband's dead body made her grieve immensely. *Wara ako kamaan, kay amo ra nga time nanawag pa tana kanakun nga mauli,* (I did not know since he still called me up earlier that he was going home), said Meg in deep sobbing. Meg was expecting her husband to be home for there were activities in town and her family would have the chance to be together again.

According to Meg, her husband was attending a birthday party as invited by one colleague. The news came through an army colleague who informed Meg's father. Worried, Meg asked the army friend what happened.

When the latter could not straightly give the details, Meg kicked and punched him forcing him to tell what had happened. The army friend simply explained that it was just a motorcycle accident and Meg's husband was slightly hurt. Not convinced still, Meg was suspicious that something serious happened to her father shouted out of dismay. Immediately that moment, her father left with the army messenger while Meg was left still worried and tremendously troubled. She kept texting her batch friends about what they knew about the accident, yet, she learned nothing from them. Late that evening, she decided to leave for Antique to bring clothes to her husband and believe that she could comfort him. Later, Meg's mother received a call from her father requesting for someone to go to Antique, whose name was very familiar to her.

That person was working at a funeral parlor, the thing that confirmed Megs' doubt about her husband's real plight. Meg found herself wildly throwing things which accidentally hit the hanging bulb. She was so upset while screaming and walking to and fro.

Daw ginagisi ang dughan ko nga di ko maman-an kun ano, gasala ako kun ano obrahun ko, daw buang lang bala ako, gadalagan ako kun diin ako maadto, as in bala daw blangko isip ko. Tanda lang gaagubay kanakun, mapalapak takun sa sarakyan bay. Mapalapak gid takun; (My heart seemed shattered into pieces. I didn't know what to do. I panicked. I was losing mind. I was like an insane running anywhere,

wanting to die, wanting for any vehicle to run over me. I was a total mess), said Meg the moment she heard of someone working in the funeral parlor.

Meg cried the whole evening. She was given a dose of tranquilizer before she was taken to the funeral parlor. Meg saw a corpse lying in army uniform and seeing him, she still could not believe it was her husband. She uttered in disbelief that anybody could wear an army uniform and it was not him, but after a closer look, and seeing her husband wearing a blue jersey sleeveless, she knew it was he, indeed, her husband. She never expected in her entire life it would happen to him. Even in her dreams, she would see he was pleading, begging for help, as Meg shared. She fully believed the death of his husband was foul play. His neck was cut, his one eye extracted. Traumatic head and neck injury was the cause of his death as Meg related.

Meg shared her experiences and struggle while grieving. When asked how she felt about the death of her husband, she said, *Blangko isip ko. Bata ko wara ko maasikaso. Pwerte ako ka niwang. Wara ako kaun-kaon. Gapakitluoy sanda kanakon nga makaon bisan gamay lang. Wara ko gakaon;* (My mind went blank. I did not pay attention to my two children. I got pale for I did not want to eat. My family convinced me to eat even a little food, yet I never took anything.)

Meg shared that she lost weight from skipping meals. She was silent most of the time. She did not mind, who visited and held vigils. She appeared unapproachable to anybody. It seemed as if she was out of her mind as if she knew no one around.

How she described the pain, she shared, *Daw ginapihak dughan ko. Daw ginahiwa bala kara nga. Sakit-sakit gid tana, as in di mo maesplikar nga sakit. Sakit sa napilasan kaw as in sakit. Asta san-o di mahukas ang pagpilas na. Di mapali;* (My heart was almost torn to pieces. It was very painful, much more painful than a deep wound that is hard to heal.) When asked how she expressed the pain, she said, *Ginahibi ko lang. Ginahibi ko lang, tapos isinggit ko;* (I cried. I cried then screamed.) Later, she would feel relieved out of this expression.

When she was asked how she felt about the loss of her husband, she replied, *Kulang. Panilag ko nawad-an ako ka sangka kahig, sangka lima, naduraan ako part kang lawas.* (It seemed a part of me died when he died; a part of me was gone and it could not be put back.)

According to Meg, she found it extremely difficult to accept the reality that her husband instantly died, as she was still expecting him to be home that day. She put the blame on some people as the cause of her husband's death. She blamed the Chief Officer, the government, even President Aquino.

Above all, she blamed God for allowing this thing to happen, for not saving his life. Meg would have accepted it if his husband got crippled and she was willing to take care of him as long as he had survived. He was expecting he would come home as he promised. But he returned home dead.

Luya katama; (Gloomy). This was how Meg described the situation days after the burial. Meg always stayed in the cemetery. He recalled what her husband told her that when he would be gone, Meg would search for another much better than he is, one who would treat her like a princess. Meg would just reply that he could never find someone much better than her husband. With this recollection, she went emotional and had thoughts of putting an end to her life. However, every time she remembered that she would just do but burst into tears, thinking of her two small children who need her attention.

There were situations that reminded Meg of her husband. When she saw families going together, she would recall her own happy family. Seeing the bear stuffed toy also reminded her of her husband for it was a precious thing to Meg. He would buy her clothes and other things she liked. Seeing anyone in army uniform also made Meg sad. Tears would automatically roll down her cheeks.

Some events that triggered Meg's sorrow include Christmas, New Year, and birthdays. Attending events like anniversaries, parties, and birthdays was no longer meaningful for Meg with the loss of her husband. Her friends would often tell her, she could survive soon, yet though she said she could, she felt weak and discouraged about how to start all over again.

Only her two kids served as her strength every time she felt down and lonely. However, on the first birthday of her child, while her husband lay in state, Meg cried hard and then let go of the pain inside her by shouting. When her grief turned to rage, she would then say, *Mabalos ako*; (I will avenge my husband's death.) She had in mind the suspect, and she plotted "revenge". She was handling her sorrow with anger. The death of his husband was so traumatic that according to Meg, it would take her more time to accept it.

It took five months for Meg to somehow gradually recover from the pain of her husband's death. She still felt the pain whenever she was alone by herself, and every time she was alone, she longed for her husband's presence.

Daad amu ja nga time imaway run kami; (We would have been together by this time) was Meg's wish. She would always carry her husband's picture. She found pleasure in her cellular phone when some of her army friends would give her a ring and a chat. Caring and compassionate words coming from her batch of

friends some what left her some comfort. Yet, after the call, she would be back to the usual grief that the loss brought her. She kept pointing accusing fingers to the suspect she had in mind as the cause of her husband's death. Yet, she had no evidence. She also blamed herself for if not for her, her husband would not have been assigned to her place. He wanted to stay closer to his family, a fact that made Meg feel guilty about her husband's death.

Syempre kun wara tana maassign ja, wara tana mapatay. Syempre kay palangga ako ka bana ko, kag gusto na man marapit tana sa pamilya namun; (Of course, if he was not assigned here, he would not have died. He loved me and he wanted to be closer to us.)

Meg remembered some unusual behavior she had upon the death of her husband. *Wara ako ti limog, hibi lang ako nga hibi. Wara ako ti ginasapak nga tawo, napabay-an ko bata ko, indi ako mabugno, ginaestorya ako pero wara ako gasabat, gaturo lang kara luha ko. Tapos daw wara ako sa sarili ko daw buang bala ako. May maabot sa balay wara ako gasur-aw kun sino bisita ko. Daw wara ako kakilala ka tawo;* (I lost my voice out of crying. I did not mind about the people coming to our house; I never entertained people. I remained silent most of the time. I was out of my mind; I seemed to lose my sanity. I seemed to know nobody).

Upon seeing other army friends coming to the funeral parlor, Meg turned to them bitterly saying,

Paano ako kaserbisyo kaninyo, bana ko patay run. Tungang gab-i ginapukaw nyo bana ko ginasundan kamo; Wara nyo gid ginbuligan bana ko nga amo run natabo kana; (How can I serve you, my husband is already dead. Where were you when he needed help? You would wake him up anytime at night and he was willing to go with you), putting the blame more on the chief officer for what happened. Meg further said that he would kill all of them out of anger and chaos.

Certain actuations were observed on Meg due to some negative thoughts she had. She admitted that she wanted to harm herself, she wanted to get killed. She recalled the vow they made to each other, *"Kay pangako namon nga darwa asta sa kamatayon mong. Ti masunod ako kana e para imaw kami nga darwa;* (We promised to love each other until the end; hence, I want to be with him.) This idea came into her mind when she was all alone by herself and deeply grieving.

To protect her from doing harsh moves, the members of the family kept an eye on her. She was advised to go out sometimes to forget her sorrow. She always went blank with the pain she could not explain. That was the most painful of all she had ever experienced, much more painful than a deep wound that could hardly be healed, was her description of the pain.

Meg expressed her grief by letting go of the tears each time she remembered her husband. After crying, she would scream. While in grief, Meg kept uttering some statements directed to God. *Naga Bana ko pa?*

Naga raku man malain nga tawo, raku man gani holdupper naga indi pa sanda? Bana ko gaserbisyo sa gobyerno, bana ko pa nga wara ti sala, bana ko pa nga buot, naga tana pa ginbuol? (Why my husband? There are a lot of evil people- robbers, why not them? Why my husband who serves the people, why him who did no wrong; he was such a good man, why him?).

The usual lines Meg would say when asked about her husband's painful death were: *Ano gid ang sala ka bana ko? Ano gid sala ka bana ko amo gid katu ang ginhimo kana?* (What wrong had he done that he was killed that way?). When asked by others of what help she wanted, Meg's sarcastic and bitter reply was, *Buhia bana ko* (Let him come to life).

Unrealized Church Vow

As a couple, Meg and her husband had many plans. One of the beautiful plans was to get married in a church. The wedding was set but he died three months before the date. He also missed his child's birthday which was a month after he got killed. He also wanted to purchase a lot for the two children. This he shared with Meg's aunt one time before the incident happened. Preparing for the children's bright future was the main concern of her husband, seeing them succeed in their studies. Seeing a car passing by, Megs' husband wanted to avail of a vehicle, and often she would tease her by saying, *Anda kara tuktukon run, atun bago pa;* (Ours would be new, while theirs would be rusty.)

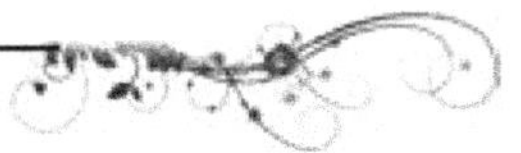

It was part of a plan, for the couple always traveled to Aklan by motorcycle. They wanted to have their own vehicle for convenience.

With the death of her husband, Meg lost some important things in life - she had lost the care of a husband she loved and enjoyed. There would be no one to provide the things she needs. The children at a young age had lost the love and care of a father. The worst effect of the death was, she had lost the only provider of their needs. She experienced financial hardship with her family.

Her Strategy for Surviving

Meg was able to cope with the loss by going out with friends. She only thought of facing life with her children. Her husband's batch mates also gave her comfort through text messages they would send her. *Ang galingaw lang kaja cell phone ko; kun manawag ang kabatch na, gapangamusta knakun, mahaw igma yapon, gapangamusta ra kanakon, tapos sanda man kra gapakadlaw*; (I find comfort in the text messages sent by his batchmates; they make me smile).

It took five months for her to somehow feel relieved, although she still cries every time she remembers her husband and the situations, or things that remind her most, *Video na, picture na, amo ra pirme,nabitbit ko*; (I always take with me his video and picture). Attending the papers to get the claim took much of her time but somehow helped alleviate her grief.

She also found relief in seeing and meeting other widows like her, *Gatugro ko advice kananda, gatugro sanda ka advice kanakon.* (We advise each other.) Her family, above all, was the source of her comfort and strength.

Story 3: Nica's Grief and Tribulation

Nica grew up in a poor family. Her mother was a plain housekeeper while her father was a fisherman. After her father died of typhoid fever, her mother found it hard to send them to school. Life was so tough for Nica's family that she wanted to help alleviate the deprived state of her brothers and sisters. Being the second child in the family and the eldest daughter, she tried to help by working in a mall in the city. She had already finished high school at that time. She helped finance her brother's education. She stayed in her aunt's house in the city. With her aunt's support, Nica was also able to go to college and finished Associate in Business Data Processing.

Nica was staying in the city when she met her life partner who was a seafarer. She was only 20 years old then while the man was 30. Seeing Nica as her kind of girl, the man did not waste a single moment showing his interest in her. He always paid her a visit and without second thoughts, he revealed his feeling. Nica, also loveless at that time, and seeing the man as responsible and kind, showed him a mutual feeling. Love bloomed between the two through constant communication. The man wrote her letters and made calls when he was back onboard the ship.

There was no opposition from Nica's mother for she saw the sincere intention of the man toward her daughter. After 18 months, the man was back home and being serious with Nica; he came to her house to ask permission to marry her. Four children were born to the couple who lived a smooth and happy life before the tragic incident happened.

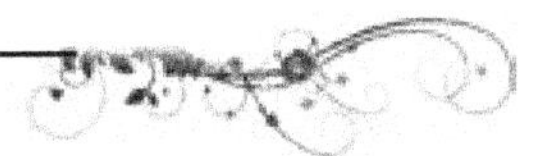

Sad Homecoming

After 13 years of a happy marriage, Nica's husband died while onboard the ship. He was two months on board when it happened. "Cardiac arrest" was the cause of her husband's death as related by the ship officer. However, according to the autopsy report, there was "foul play" surrounding his death as shown in the hematoma on his waist. Nica believed that someone or some unidentified shipmates could have beaten her husband in his cabin.

The news reached Nica at noontime while she was nursing her two-month-old baby. Nica received two calls, first from the shipmaster, then, from the office personnel. Nica was reluctant to take the news for it was like a bomb in her ear; she got tongue-tied hearing the unexpected message. Nica narrated that a commotion was heard in his husband's cabin. The crew tried knocking at his door, but there was no reply; they kept calling him on the intercom, but to no avail; hence, they were forced to open the door using the master key. They found him lying on his bed lifeless. They tried patting him to wake him up, but he never responded. He was given first aid because he still had a heartbeat, and rising blood pressure of 200/90. But after four hours, he was not revived.

With the astounding news, Nica's first reaction was to cry, *Naghibi ako eh, ang nabatyagan ko daw indi ako magpati, tapos, mu tu naghibi ako, tapos, hambal ko basi indi pa ra tuod;*

(I cried and I could hardly believe it. It might not be true.) Nica's heart seemed like it was being pierced while tears rolled down her face. She wept bitterly in disbelief that this could happen to her husband who had just called her a week before. He had just gone back onboard and this suddenly happened. She was deeply saddened by the news.

The pain she felt was beyond measure, according to Nica. She wept while she imagined her helpless husband fighting for life in the middle of the sea. It took days for the ship to go offshore and had it been earlier, Nica thought that her husband could have survived. The thought that foul play happened was also unbearable to accept. Doubts, despair, and bitterness wrapped up her heart and mind. All she could do was to cry terribly, *Daw indi ako magpati, tapos, mu tu naghibi ako, garing di gid ako kapatama; wara gid ako gapatama.* (I could hardly believe it. I cried hard. But I had to remain calm.)

Nica was given a tranquilizer for her to stay calm. The family was worried about her health, she had just delivered a baby whom she breastfed. Nica kept reiterating her disbelief that it was not her husband who died but somebody else. She kept entertaining the thought that it was a big mistake that her husband died. This denial was coupled with overflowing tears.

When the lifeless body of her husband arrived at the mortuary, Nica dared not to see it. She did not even come near it. For her, it was the saddest homecoming. She grieved in a corner while the body was brought in.

She only went there to sign the autopsy account. She immediately left after signing the document needed.

Nine days of obsequies led Nica to deep sorrow and disheartening thought that *daad wara lang mapatay*, (wish he had not died.) Despite the presence of the mourners who came, she felt herself shrinking in deep sorrow and denial about the death of her husband. She ignored the people who came to the vigil. She would stay in her room and lamented alone.

Deep sadness contained Nica's world, days after her husband's interment. She felt the deep sorrow and emptiness brought by the loss of her husband. Too many things reminded her of him. Her children greatly reminded her of him, especially the recent baby who looked exactly like him. Seeing her children eased up her longing for her husband. She could not imagine life without him. Nica said she would miss what they used to do when her husband was home, like going shopping in the mall, playing, and having fun in the house. Seeing the car left unused and the poultry project he enjoyed while home reminded her of his presence. Hearing the phone ringing also tormented her. She would expect her husband's call each month. She reminisced how her husband would give reminders to their children and his nagging on the phone if she answered the call late. On the other hand, Nica admitted she was bitter with her husband's crew who failed to help him survive. She just prayed to overcome the ill feelings toward them.

She just took vitamins in order to sleep well and she said she somehow had better sleep after that. She even experienced having overslept.

Unfulfilled Dreams

Nica and her husband had some plans. To repair their house was one. Their top priority was their children's future. For Nica, her children's future was the most important so she kept reminding her husband to open a bank account for each of them. To save for them was their goal starting that year, but unfortunately, he died.

To pay for a lot was also part of their plan. Her husband agreed that he would limit the call so as to save for their children.

Sometimes, Nica would ask herself some questions and would give herself answers, *Ano gaba run ja? Ano challenge ja knakon?* (Is this a curse? Is this a challenge?) Nica would immediately hold on to the thought that God probably loved her husband, the reason why He took him away. Yet she wished, *Daad wara lang napatay; daad kun napatay gid man, indi lang tulad nga gagmay pa kabataan ko;* (I wished he did not die yet, not this time when my kids are still small.) These were the common thoughts that came into her mind when she was alone. She also had thoughts of running away to escape from reality.

With the pain of loss, Nica wanted to have a new environment, forget the memories, and escape from things that made her angry. She shared that she had problems with her in-laws. She had a misunderstanding with them, especially with the issue of "money". She wanted to go into business or work. She could not decide for herself without the intervention of her husband's family, especially on money matters. This idea surfaced after the burial.

While Nica was not yet a widow, she openly shared financial help with their needy neighbors. After the loss, she stopped helping or sharing. Nica said that since her husband passed away, she received nothing; hence, she had to be extra wise with spending the money her husband had left her. She was jobless so she had to be prudent enough to handle the financial resources intended for her children.

Some of her routine activities had changed. She seldom went shopping or bought clothes and toys for her little children. She used to do those monthly, after getting the allotment, she would spend time going around the mall, buying the things they needed, and sometimes on things that pleased her. After the loss, she set some limitations and prioritized "first thing first".

The loss of her husband mainly affected her budget. Although she admitted she had enough at that time, she found the change in spending the money. She delegated everything to her husband as regards money. For her children, the death was a big loss, the fact that they became "fatherless". This made Nica shed more tears while sharing. Her statements were sort of intermittent utterances. Nica had to decide everything for the family. She lost the most important thing she calls the "love of a husband", no more phone ringing from a husband away from home; this made her weep further. When asked about sexual need, she simply replied that she never yearned for it since she was under the shadow of intense grief over the loss. She never thought about it because of the overwhelming pain.

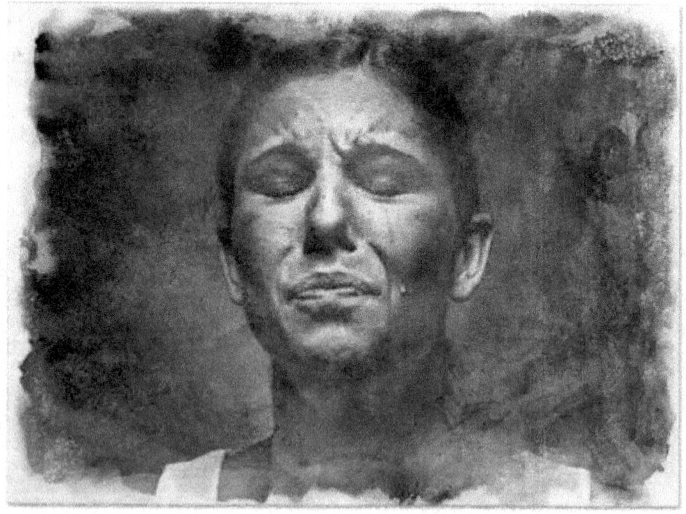

Finding Comfort during Hard Times

Shedding tears helped every time Nica remembered the loss. Spending more time with her children and attending to their daily needs helped her cope. She would pray every time she recalled the painful death of her husband. Nica became more depressed days after the burial. She said so because she could not see her husband anymore. For three months, Nica wept heavily. She would only stop crying when she became busy with her children's needs in school. She would remember the grief when her children would ask about their father. It was difficult to explain to them the reality of death. Her children served as a comfort to her grieving heart. For them, she tried to cope with her sadness. Nica's environment also helped during her severe bereavement. She was exposed to an environment where there were many people coming to her house. She would huddle with the visitors around; some of whom are close relatives and friends. Every afternoon, people would gather to play "bingo." These were the times when she would be relieved of her depressive episodes. But when she was alone, she would cry.

Story 4: Ella's Pain and Sorrow

Almost twenty years in service as a teacher made Ella a fulfilled person. It was through this profession that she was able to meet her partner in life. That was when she transferred to Antique to teach for two years that she met the man of her life.

Without a doubt, after seeing each other, a relationship bloomed and later they decided to get married. They moved to Ella's place and built their home. Ella was assigned to teach in a barrio, just two rides away from her house. Two children, a girl, and a boy were born to Ella. Her husband, being a ship officer, and she, as a teacher, lived a good life. The house was a two-storey, concrete type in a vast area in the *poblacion*. At first glimpse of her, she seemed to be a typical woman, yet visiting her mansion and knowing her well would leave an impression of her as a person of humility and simplicity.

Soft-spoken, warm, and approachable were the common apparent characteristics that she also possessed. She was a homebody, diligent, and hard-working. She lived with her two children and only sister at home. She was preparing for a school evaluation during the first meeting.

A genial smile welcomed the researcher as she opened the gate with the willingness to share about her life and experiences as a widow.

Like the rest, she started with a s mile and curiosity but later the happy aura suddenly changed to gloom in a rough voice as she unveiled the sad events in her life.

The Torment

One common instance for wives with husbands who are OFWs is receiving a long-distance call anytime. For Ella, she never expected that one midnight, she would receive a strange call that would break her heart and bring devastation to her entire life. The call came from the office informing them that her husband had a cardiac arrest and was not able to survive. It was such a piece of fatal news to hear in the middle of the night when everyone else at home was peacefully sleeping.

Ella was not upset by the phone ringing at that time, only, that to her expectation, she would hear her husband's voice; instead, a woman's voice was on the line, personnel of his office in Manila. She then started to doubt. Later, the woman asked how they had been with her children and what she observed regarding her husband's health. Her doubt heightened that something was wrong with him and later she was informed that her husband had a heart attack in his cabin.

Nabuy-an ko dayon telepono kag magnguyngoy; Wara ko ginpadayon run kay dayad run pamatyag ko mong, gakudog ang lawas ko. Nguyngoy lang ako nga nguyngoy; (I dropped the phone and I drooped and fell down on my knees and

cried. My whole body was trembling.) Ella did not remember anymore what else the woman had said for she started to get weak and helpless while the phone was left hanging. From past twelve midnight until the morning, she was sleepless, crying all by herself.

Ella was 49 when her husband succumbed to cardiac arrest on board the ship. Her husband had just returned to sea service and before he left, all medical results were clear so it had never been in Ella's mind that it would happen to his husband. At that time, his husband was 60 and he had plans of retiring after the next sea service.

Morning broke with deep mourning for Ella's children upon knowing that their father had died. His relatives in Antique already knew the sad news.

The corpse was taken to Antique. *Subo*; (Sad) this was what Ella said when asked how she felt about the news. *Naga ikaw pa mayad ikaw sa mga tawo, kabuot kanimo, naga ikaw pa? Ang iban jan nga indi mapuslan, wara ginuna, amo ra bala. Naga ikaw pa nga kinanglan ka pa ka mga tawo*; (Why him? Of all people, why him who is good? Many people expect for his help, why him?) All these desperate utterances came out of Ella's lips.

The corpse was transferred to and buried in Miagao. Sorrow and emptiness embraced Ella's days after the burial. All that was left to her were sad and happy memories of her husband. She remembered what he usually did, what he told his children, the advice, and their good times together as a complete family going out shopping, eating, and enjoying the presence of each other when he was home.

Ella never expected it to happen since a week before the accident, they still talked over the phone and everything went smoothly. She believed that her husband got stressed with the work for they were about to have a drydock. Much work had to be done and that might have affected her husband's physical condition at that time. Ella resorted to tears and more tears during the next days of her life. Sometimes, she blamed the other crew for not taking him to the nearest hospital or any means that would have helped him survive. Every time she remembered the event where her husband was alone and away from his family, Ella felt sadness.

Ella's husband decided to have the last contract, then retire from the job considering his age. He would just wait for a yearly pension from the company while managing the rice land they have acquired in Antique. In Ella's mind, she kept repeating the question "why my husband" and he blamed God for allowing it when he could have still helped other people.

During the wake, Ella went blank as if he did not mind who came for condolences. She seemed to have a mental block of the situation. She felt uninterested to talk to anybody. When she went back to teaching, at first, she felt lazy. Sometimes, she would go out because she felt so bad. She would pause a while; she would forget her sorrow if she focused on small children. Later, she found herself in the midst of sadness. She would teach momentarily, then she was back to silence and inner struggle of depressive episodes. She isolated herself from colleagues who would gather in groups for a chat with her. She avoided the thought of grieving, yet deep inside she mourned. She had no interest in associating with others. She just wanted to be alone.

There was no change in Ella's usual routine. She did the same daily tasks - attending to her children's needs, home chores, and classroom teaching. There was not much effect on the finances she said the claim was enough for her children's future. What she had in mind was how she could bring up the children, a responsibility she found quite difficult. She had to accustom herself to disciplining her children as a single parent.

For Ella, life is different with a father in the family. A father's discipline is different and firm and a father figure was what the children wanted and longed for. The children missed their father so much as she shared.

For her, nothing could replace the most important thing in her life as the *Pagpalangga kang sangka bana sa asawa*; (love of a husband for a wife). For Ella, love was the most important thing she had lost since her husband had been taken away by God. Her world became gloomy being alone and grieving. In her bereavement, she lost weight, especially after the burial. She felt the emptiness that she could not hold back her tears, especially when someone came and talked about her husband.

Still, moments like birthdays, anniversaries, and going to work reminded her of her husband. When teaching, she would think of her husband, especially when she was with her colleagues talking about "family life and trouble."

Kun may bana kaw, obligado ikaw; ang bana kabay gusto na man nga atipanon mo man; magrigos, ready mo mga bayo na kun may adtunan; manindahan, mahimos, magkaon; (If you have a husband, you have to take care of him, his needs, bath, clothes, food, when going to the market.) These were the tasks she used to do for her husband and now being a widow, she no longer does all these things.

Forgetting the Grief

It took a year for Ella to recover from the loss. She would prefer to stay alone than go out somewhere. Being a homebody, she would stay at home and watch TV. She would go out only once in a while. She seldom went on vacation or shopping for pleasure to forget her grief. Her own simple way of taking time with her children, teaching, and doing household tasks - helped her out of sadness.

Seeing other widows and sharing their grief somewhat gave her a feeling of relief and comfort. To avoid having negative thoughts, Ella just imagined that her husband was on board as she was already used to situations when her husband was always away for months, sometimes for more than a year. These have become common to her. In order to move on, her children inspired her as a widow, so she took care of herself so as not to get sick for their sake.

Story 5: Belen, Scarred by Bereavement

Belen was a simple person with a simple dream in life. She was born to a poor family, a daughter of a farmer and a housekeeper. Because of poverty, Belen was not able to pursue college; however, as a high school graduate, she was hired as a hotel attendant, a way for her to earn and somehow help her impoverished family. In that workplace, she met her lifetime soul mate who was a security guard. After four months of a romantic relationship, the two decided to get married. Year after year, a child was born to Belen and her husband. They finally bore eight, seven girls and one boy, who were raised simply through farming, carpentry, housekeeping, and laundry. In the midst of life's hardship, the couple was able to send all eight children to school. To seek better earnings, the family moved to the place of Belen's husband.

The husband worked as a carpenter in a big rest house, also owned by his cousin living abroad. The income was augmented through farming and other part-time work in the barangay. The family stayed in the rest house, at the same time, worked as caretakers. In this setting, the couple produced three professionals. Belen also acknowledged that they got support from her husband's close relatives while serving as house caretakers.

Belen's 27 years of a happy marriage was disrupted by the unexpected sudden death of her husband in a motorcycle accident. The husband was driving back home after taking the two children to

school. He was on his way home when a six-wheeler truck sideswiped the motorcycle he was driving. While trying to avoid a dog on the highway, the fast-running truck overtaking behind hit his motorcycle. It made the motorcycle lose its control and slide into the roadway. With the impact, Belen's husband was thrown off the motorcycle and broke his head.

The news about the accident reached Belen. Her attention was first focused on her two children with the thought that the husband only had a minor injury. When she confirmed that the children safely reached school, she was relieved. As for her husband, she thought that it would be mere scratches on the legs, and there was nothing serious to be upset of. Still, she left with a relative to see her husband who, according to the report, was taken to the hospital. Worry gripped Belen's heart when she passed by the scene of the incident and saw the people gathered. She paused, wanting to come closer to the area, but she was stopped by a relative accompanying her. She was told it was just the wrecked motorcycle remains the people were witnessing, nothing more. It gave Belen a sigh of relief and altogether, they went back to the rest house. Later, Belen's five children arrived home. They were serious while controlling the tears to show her that nothing happened. Shortly, the children came near her and without hesitation, they bravely told their mother the truth, *Nay, relax ka lang, Nay ha, a pagkamatuod, patay na si tatay*; (Nay, please stay relaxed, the truth is, Tatay died in that accident.)

These words exploded like a bomb in Belen's ears. Tears flowed, hearing the painful truth that her children just said.

Sagad lang ako kahibi kag daw indi ko mabaton eh, ano bala gulpiyada; (I cried. It seems, I could hardly accept it. It was a sudden death.) These were Belen's statements on the revelation about the death of her husband. She further said, *Paano na lang kami, o kaday ah nga daw masakit man batyagon; ano bala nga madura tana sa gulpyada tapos duro pa kabataan namun?* (What would life be without him? I am left in deep pain with eight children.)

Seeing the dead body at the funeral made Belen weep bitterly as if she could not accept the fact that her husband had died painfully. Tears and more tears were shed in the next days and nights in Belen's life. How she pitied her husband having died with a broken head. It was such a painful memory for her to recall as she shared.

Belen and her husband would usually stay or sleep in their cottage

Wrestling with Grief

Days after the burial, Belen kept weeping over the loss of her husband. Some things and situations reminded her and made her cry. She imagined her children getting home with him coming from school. The sound of the motorcycle he was driving signaled that the children were coming. When someone approached the rest house driving a motorcycle, Belen would stop working and sit down thinking about her husband. She started letting go of her tears as she realized he was dead. The cottage facing the sea where her husband would usually stay or have a get-together with some friends also reminded her of the past. Her husband would drink with his friends in that cottage and she could see the exact area where he would sit and talk with friends while having a drink with them.

Sometimes, they would sleep in that cottage. Seeing a gun also made her sob again and again. Seeing the roving *tanods* with guns revived the memories she had with her husband who was once a *tanod,* too. When she passed by the scene of the incident, she would just utter a statement as if her husband was there still, *Tatay, maagi lang ako Tatay*; (Tatay, I will just pass by.)

The birthday anniversary, most of all, was a painful memory for he died before his birthday. They had a plan to celebrate the birthday and would invite some of his friends and one high-ranking military official in town.

The anniversary was very sad for Belen because the birthday which was meant to be happy became a very sad one, brought about by the tragic accident.

Belen understood that it was an accident and it was nobody's fault. However, she admitted that some questions to God came into her mind, *Lord, ngaa ginbuol mo dayun ang bana ko nga duro pa amon nga saragudon? Di ko pa kaya, duro pa paeskwelahon ko;* (Lord, why did you take his life so suddenly when I am helpless with eight children? They are still going to school.)

On the other hand, guilt somewhat haunted her. She believed that had she stopped her husband from leaving early, he would not have died. With the loss of her husband, Belen said, *Temprano pa nabul-an ako ka bana.* (I became a widow at this age. She found life hard with the death of her husband.) Makaestoryahanay kami kun ano ang problema; (We could talk about our problem.)

She recalled her unusual actuations and thoughts she recalled she had been: *Sangkabulan, daw masinggit kaw. Wara ka run sa sakto nga kaisipan, wara gaatindir sa iban tawo. May bes nga gapanaw kaw, wala sa kaisipan, lain mabutang. Masugud ikaw, lain ang maobra, kis-a, gaprito ako, lain ruman, gahugas kaw pinggan eh, tapos, matig-ang gali ako, kis a, makislan ko dun, lain takuri ruman ibutang ko, isun- ad ko tu sa kalayo, gali ang kaldero ngara may sulod, abi mo nabalunasan mo dun, indi mo masun-ad kay nalipatan mo bala haw.* (I wanted to shout. I was out of my mind. I did not mind about other people.

Sometimes, I went blank. I put things in different places when I started working, I would do another task; Sometimes, I could not imagine what I was working on, which one I would finish first. I would forget what to do.)

Belen often dreamt of him as if alive. She would wake up in tears and realize it was just a dream. This enhanced her longing for her husband, yet, there was relief, too. *Pagbugtaw ko abi ko matuod, nasubuan ko kay indi gali tuod. Mayad gawa pamatyag ko, nakita mo mong. Kaagi gid gani ako kadamgo nga isip ko buhi gid kuno, kuon nanda patay gid tana, nami kuno estoryahanay namun, gapungko ako, buhay- buhay napiyungan ako, nakapisik ako, ay damgo ko lang gli tu!* (When I woke up, I thought it was real, I felt sad because it was just a dream. Yet, I felt better, too, seeing him in my dream. He was as if he were alive in my dream. They said he was dead, yet, there I saw him and we talked…later, I woke up it was, indeed, a dream!)

At first, Belen felt the happiness her dream brought her, but later, she would cry, miss his presence. For Belen, the most painful part of grieving was knowing the death of her husband. This was due to the fact that it was a very painful death that his husband had. It took four months for Belen to accept the truth of his passing. Days after the burial was full of loneliness for, she said, she no longer saw him.

Lain gid man gali kun wara kaw ti bana, wara kaw ti estoryahon, waay timbang sa pagpangabuhi ninyo, waay paangga-anggaan. As balo, bakas-bakas ka run eh, ifocus mo gid sa pagpangabuhi; Kun jan tana, bisan indi kaw mag-obra. Kun balo kaw, lain gid pamatyagan, gakaurungan ako, kalain ang mabatyagan. Hinali lang madumduman mo ang ginapanghimo na kanimo, ang pagpalangga na kanimo, pag-atipan na kun may balatian ikaw; Sa kabataan, syempre gapawala lang ako kay jan si tatay da, kun magpinaugtas sanda, jan si tatay nanda, disiplina ka kabataan; Kauna sa kabataan, makitatay sanda, daw wala ako sang una galaygay, gasarig ako sa tatay nanda, si tatay nanda lang galaygay; Maninda, si tatay da manindahan, tilad ako run; (Life of a widow is different. There is no one to talk to, no helpmate, and no one to care for you. As a widow, you have to double your effort. If he is still here, I can sometimes rest from working hard. If you're a widow, it is a different feeling, sometimes, you get blank, you will always recall what he used to do in the family; there is no one to take care of your needs when you get sick.... I turned over the responsibility to their father, the discipline, which for now, I am doing. I seldom gave advice to my children for it was my husband who did it. Now, I have to do it. Their father did the marketing, now that he's gone; I have to take the responsibility.)

The situation of having no husband around was difficult for Belen working as a caretaker. Everything had a limit. *Kis-a naisip ko nga daw guba na ang pagpangabuhi ko kay wara run mong. Syempre naisip ko nga guba na, ang mga plano namun;* (Sometimes, I have thought, our life and plans are hopeless since he passed away), the thoughts that made Belen sadder. With the loss of her husband, Belen wanted to leave and go back to her own home with her children. She found life too different without her husband, *Kauna nga buhi tana, bisan turogturog, batang-batang kaw wala kaw mabatian nga estorya, namayha kaw di mag-obra;* (While he was yet alive, you can sleep if you want, now you can't do it, you have to work.) Belen and her husband had a dream to realize. This was to save money to redeem a mortgaged lot and later could build a house of their own. It was Belen's ardent desire to have a house where she could gather all her children together and live simply and happily. She wanted to imagine living under a roof where they would eat together and have fun together while she prepared food for her family. Belen wanted all her children to be educated and each to have a better life. Another personal wish she had was to go back to her own place with her children and to have a house of their own.

Her Source of Hope and Comfort

Belen found comfort in her children who are her sources of strength and inspiration to face the life of widowhood. With them, she was able to cope with the grief caused by the death of her husband. Her children would take her to the city and this greatly helped her in coping with her sorrow. Sometimes, chatting with her husband's close relatives comforted her, too. Watching TV somehow also alleviated her sadness. Although being a widow is disheartening, yet, Belen acknowledged she has gained strength in seeing others overcome the same grief she has experienced.

Story 6: Death is an Appointment:
Rosa's Grief

Rosa experienced grief over her husband's death when she was in her late 60s. She herself was not feeling well at the time it happened. She never expected the time was up for her husband who showed no symptoms of illness that early morning of December while preparing to attend an "Aguinaldo" mass. Rosa's husband woke up early to attend the mass with her but she decided to stay because she did not feel well. The husband, described by Rosa as "religious" or prayerful, did not want to miss the "Aguinaldo." He went on his way walking to the church which was a few meters away from their house. Often, the couple would ride on a tricycle but at that time, being alone, he walked. A passing vehicle actually offered a ride yet he refused since he wanted to take a walk. When he reached the church, he had just sat down when he suddenly fainted. Immediately, he was rushed to a clinic, just a few meters away from the church. The physician pronounced him dead on arrival, a victim of cardiac arrest.

Rosa was informed by a neighbor about what had happened and immediately, she hurried to the emergency clinic where her husband was rushed for first aid. *Wara gid ako kahibi. Daw indi ako magpati dasun nagkudog lang ako. Man-an ko patay run. Daw gasakay ako sa panganod, gakurudog ang lawas ko, gakurunos. Man-an ko kay gakudog ang kahig ko kag baba ko.* (I felt numb and floating. I just felt my knees were shaking. I was speechless. In my mind were varied thoughts that I could not remember.).

The Pain of Losing a Soul Mate

Rosa only started to shed tears when her husband's brothers and sisters arrived at the scene. She was given a relaxant to lower her blood pressure. Rosa's sadness was plainly shown in the silence of seeing her husband in the coffin. She did not cry much, she said, but she admitted she was deeply saddened by the reality that her husband had died. She started feeling deep grief days after the burial. She could hardly accept the fact that he had left her completely. She cried every time she was alone and recalled the sad and happy memories with him.

A lot of things kept reminding her, *Daw nagahinulsol kaw kang una mo nga sala kana. Ginaaway ko pa, slight man lang, pareho kara sa sulod ka balay kun buhay tana kakaon kundi mauna ako. Daw indi ako magbugno kana*; (I seemed to regret all what I had done him. Sometimes I quarreled with him, especially if I would call him to eat and he would ignore me. I would not talk to him, either.) Remembering this, Rosa would start sobbing. *Naluoy ako kana, nga ridya timo gakaun, galantaw ka TV, tana sara lang sa lungon amo ra bala haw*; (I pity him thinking he is alone in his coffin, while I eat or watch TV.)

More than once Rosa uttered, *Patawarun lang ang mga sala na, ang kalag na dar-un sa langit*; (God forgive his sins and his soul may be taken to heaven), then later, she sobbed again. Tears flowed down after she missed seeing her husband

in the house. She grieved for almost a year and letting go of her tears was her way of expressing the grief. *Gahibi lang ako, mayad pa gani kun makahibi ako*, (I just cried. I feel better when I have cried.)

During the grief, one strange event she recalled was, she went home as if she did not know where her house was. She just found herself home. Three months after the burial, one of the unforgettable moments happened when Rosa went with her friends to a get-together. She drank seven bottles of beer which made her intoxicated. Quite unaware of what she was doing, she danced on top of the table while her friends would laugh at her. She was with her cousins so she did not mind it at all. Yet, it gave her some kind of relief. When asked if she would do the same if her husband were alive; *Indi ko man tu paghimuon kun buhi bana ko*; (I would never do such a thing if my husband were alive.)

Daw useless ang tanan; (life seems useless) was Rosa's description of her situation being a widow. *Kis-a daw useless gid kun maguli kaw nga wara tana jan, magkaon nga ikaw lang sara*; (Sometimes it is useless, especially when you get home and he's not there, especially when you eat alone.)

With smile, she further said, *Nami daad kis a nga galoving-loving kamo, galantaw ka TV daad. Nami daad may bana kaw* ….(It is good if there is someone teasing you….watching TV together. It is good having a husband.)

When she heard the word "balo" (widow), she never got offended, yet, she felt empty being alone, she said, *Mayad ruman ra kun sa crowd kaw* (It is good if you're already in the crowd.)

Tears followed when she remembered her husband. When she would attend the mass alone, she cried especially in recalling that her husband died in the church. Seeing the grapes and "lupi nga pilit" reminded her of their husband's favorite food which she used to buy every time she went to the market. At night, before praying, Rosa recalled the moment and later she cried again. This happened after a year of grieving.

Rosa found being alone quite hard, especially when problems with the children arose. She said that if her husband were alive, he would be there to settle or to help. With regard to finances, she did not find it a problem at all since she was also receiving her monthly pension.

One important goal that her husband missed to realize was building her a better house. This was the plan of her husband together with their children who have jobs. Her husband also convinced her to go on a tour to other countries, yet, she refused because of her physical condition and fear of traveling. Yet, remembering all these made her smile about her husband whom she said was a loving partner.

Overcoming Loneliness

Pangamuyo (Prayers) helped Rosa cope with her grief. This was her great weapon in times of sadness. She still cried every time she remembered her husband. She was thankful for the presence of her children and grandchildren who have served as comfort, too. Every three months, she joined her circle of friends in a get-together, a way for her to be happy in the midst of widowhood. This, for her, gives meaning to her life.

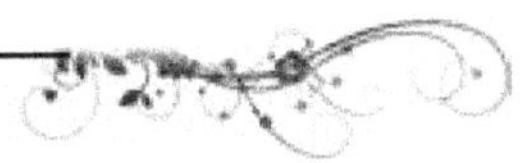

Story 7: Angel's Tempest Toss

Angel was born to a family of middle-class status. Her father (deceased) was a field employee while her mother was a teacher. She was an only child but she had some stepbrothers from her father's first family. Her mother was a second wife, but she did not grow up with her. Instead, she was taken care of by her aunt to whom she was more attached.

Angel finished Bachelor of Arts major in Psychology. After graduating from college, she immediately worked in one of the malls in the city. She had served as a consigner clerk for seven years, then later, was called to teach in a college. Her partner in life had been her close friend since high school. After some years of being apart, she met him again. Angel had been praying for him to be her lifetime partner, and that wish became a reality. However, having different religious beliefs, they took their vows through a civil wedding. The young couple lived a simple life together with their child who was a girl.

In the first few months of being together, Angel's husband did not have a stable job; hence, he was the one taking care of the child. When the need arose, they would seek the help of their parents from both sides. Later, the husband was also able to get a job with Angel's help. He worked as an appliance salesman in the city.

Life for Angel and her husband went well with one child. The two were starting to build more dreams and wishes as a family when the tragedy happened. Angel was then 29 years old.

The Mishap

Hours before the tragedy, Angel and her husband were together. The two were planning to buy a motorcycle. But the plan was canceled because it was a holiday. Instead, the couple went together for snacks. The day was a memorable one with her husband buying her t-shirts as gifts. Angel realized it was the last moment she had with her husband. Angel was left in the mall to work while her husband went home ahead. The two agreed to see each other at night.

In the place of Angel's husband, somebody died. He then asked permission to spend vigil hours together with a friend of the bereaved family. Since it was already dark, her husband decided to stay overnight. He informed Angel through a text message that he would sleep in the place. Angel, who was already waiting, encouraged him to go home although late. Finally, her husband decided to go home. He took a ride home on a motorcycle with a friend.

Worry gripped Angel while waiting for her husband who said he was home in a few minutes, yet he never appeared.

A text message from her sister-in-law came instead, informing her that her husband, together with a friend, met in a motorcycle accident. The two were taken to the nearest hospital.

Angel was told to go to the hospital as soon as possible, and with this, she became more upset. Angel, starting to panic as if she did not know what to do, called her mother who was staying in the city. She hired a vehicle to take her to a hospital she was not yet sure where. She passed by the scene of the incident and seeing the pieces of the motorcycle strewn about and splattered with blood in the roadway added to her worry. She felt nauseous and more anxious because she could not stand taking a long glimpse of the area. Another text message came after the other needed her presence in the hospital.

According to the story, Angel's husband was riding on his friend's motorcycle heading home when another motorcycle suddenly approached and accidentally the two motorcycles collided head-on. The drivers were all thrown off the motorcycle due to the impact of the head-on collision. The other motorcycle driver died on the spot. The news that first reached Angel was that her husband just had a minor injury from falling down the motorcycle. With this in mind, she said, *Blangko pa ko… daw ginkulbaan ako. Sa mind ko ginrush tana sa city kay di kumpleto ang facilities sa Guimbal,* (I went blank, I got nervous. In my mind I thought he was transferred to the city for better facilities.)

Angel became more worried knowing that her husband's friend died. She had in mind that perhaps the friend died because he was the one driving the motorcycle while her husband was only slightly hurt.

While she was on her way to the hospital in the city, text messages kept buzzing, and these enhanced her worry. A text message saying that her husband "had passed away" made her utter sadly, *Indi ra tuod, Indi ra tuod*; (It is not true! It is not true!)

Along the way, Angel wanted to cry but she held back the tears until she saw her husband's dead body. When she reached the hospital, she first saw her mother waiting at the entrance of the emergency room. Angel's mother told her to calm down. She finally revealed that her husband had died from the accident. *Man-an ko run ra mang;* (I knew it already, Mama), she said in a downcast voice.

Upon seeing her mother's reaction as if to break down, Angel also cried saying, *Naga wara na ako ginhulat....Daad may last pa nga ginhambal,* (Why didn't he wait for me, I should have heard his last words) Angel seemed down on her knees while saying these words. When asked about her initial reactions, she said, *Indi takun magpati.* (I didn't believe it!)

She burst into tears as if blaming someone for the cause of the death. Some questions were in her mind, *Naga bala haw, naga wara ko gintaw-an ti time?* (Why? Why was I not given a chance?)

Angel's husband died just a few seconds before she arrived. She regretted she came late to see her husband. The *barangay tanod* who rushed him to a hospital handed her the wedding ring. With this, Angel could no longer hold back her tears.

She cried hard, shouting, *Indi ra tuod, Indi ra tuod!* (It is not true! It is not true!)Angel went inside the emergency clinic and glanced at her husband's dead body. He looked as if he was only sleeping; yet, his body was as hard as wood when she touched him. *Nag-uy-oy ako, nagpungko ko sa kilid kag magpisngu-pisngo ko pero indi ko kahibi;* (I fell down on my knees and started to sob, but I could not cry hard enough).

The motorcycle reminded Angel of her husband's painful death.

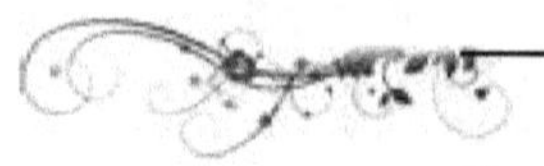

Days of Desolation

Angel's husband died of internal hemorrhage from the motorcycle head-on collision. In the midst of deep sorrow, she still managed to report to her work to settle e matters. She felt as if no tears would fall. She felt numb. She only burst into tears when her close friends started hugging her for condolences. Somehow, seeing them gave her much comfort.

Every night she told her mother, Mama, *daw di ko kamaan maghibi;* (Mama, I don't know how to cry.) She felt as if numb days after the death of her husband.

After the burial, Angel found herself grieving deeply, especially when certain things or events reminded her of her husband. Their little girl who resembles her father reminded Angel of her husband's presence. Each time she took a ride on the jeepney she and her husband used to ride; she could not help but let her tears flow. To avoid the painful memory, she would ride in another vehicle. Seeing some of his husband's best friends also made her sadder. How she wished he were still alive to see them. At home, she would imagine him sitting in a place while watching TV. A motorcycle passing by would cause her much anguish and she would feel a rapid heartbeat recalling the tragic accident met by her husband. Angel would sigh in deep sorrow whenever she saw a painted landscape.

The painting was her husband's hobby and artistic skill. She said he promised to give her a blue rose.

So, during the burial, Angel prepared even an artificial rose painted blue since this was her husband's favorite which he failed to give to Angel because he had died.

Angel was able to land a teaching job practicing her field in psychology. On her first day in school, she was reminded of a female colleague driving a motorcycle. She dared remind her to be careful in driving as she revealed her husband's fatal accident. One time, she said, while she was walking home from church, she was offered a ride on a motorcycle by her husband's best friend. She hesitated, yet, she was forced to ride, *Nagpirong ako, raw-ay ang feeling ko.* (I just closed my eyes, I felt nervous.) She seldom rides on a motorcycle because of the event. For Angel, the loss of her husband was the most unwanted event in her life, *Naduraan ako ti friend, wara run ako ti comfort. Kun jan lang tana secure ang pamatyag ko;* (I lost a friend, a comforter. I feel secure if he is there.) On the death of her husband, Angel's mind set in, Wara run, wara run ti tsansa, (There's no more chance.)

This she meant saying before her mother, *Maano na lang ako kaja bay? May gana ka pa kaja wara run ang tawo gabulig gapastrong kanimo;* (What should I do? I lost hope since I lost the person who gives me strength.) She wanted to say something else but she could not put across what was in her heart. She admitted that she felt angry when she heard her mama say that her husband had died. This anger was associated with her regret of having missed talking to her husband at the last minute of his life. She was angry

that she never heard any word from her husband before he departed. She was angry at herself too, knowing she argued with him before the accident happened, yet her husband still tried to go home as she wanted. If she did not convince him to go home, her husband would not have died in that accident, she thought.

On the other hand, guilt also haunted her, *daad ginpasugtan ko na lang maturog tana sa anda lugar. Daad kun nadelay lang ti gamay, ginkagat ka lasga daad, little something nga nagprevent;* (I would have allowed him to sleep there for if he stayed, it never happened or there was a delay, as if he was bitten by an ant, something like that could have prevented his plan to leave.)

Folks around encouraged her to move on for she was still young, especially since she has a child. This encouraged and comforted Angel a lot. She just felt sad about her child, especially on the first few days after the interment; the child had a nightmare looking for her father. Angel would again start crying with the thought, *Makita ikaw ka tatay mo kun ano ikaw kabahol tulad.* (Your father would see how you have grown.) Angel remembered what her husband could have said the moment before he passed away.

She would find it difficult to take care of the child. She had to manage everything for the child and for herself all alone. She felt sad being alone sitting outside, recalling how they talked of anything, petty and important things.

When asked what she would do when she felt sad, she replied, *Gasulat.* (I write.) To forget the memories which made her cry again and again. Angel said that she covered the picture of her husband on the wall. This was to forget her grief over the pain of his death.

Angel and her husband were hoping to have another child, particularly a boy. They were planning to have a church wedding, too, to build a house of their own, to buy and raise animals.

To buy a motorcycle to serve as transportation was their priority. These thoughts gave Angel some pain, for the motorcycle was the cause of her husband's death.

Finding Strength and Hope

It was good that Angel was working because she was able to recover fast. It took her from six months to one year to overcome her grief. The grief would be at its peak when she would find herself alone with her child. Somehow, her child is her source of comfort and joy. She just imagined that her husband went abroad. Through people around reaching out, she was able to forget her sadness. Some of her

friends would take her out for comfort. Old folks also reminded her to be strong for her child. Seeing her mother and aunt as widows somehow gave her comfort and strength, *Pareho run kita nga mga widows, different variations, kamo mal -am nabalo, ako bata pa nabalo*; (We have the same situation now as widows, but we got widowed at different ages.)

Story 8: Maria's Pain and Lamentation

Being born to a poor family, Maria lived a life described as "hand to mouth". She had to work hard in order to survive. She lived in a small bamboo hut without electricity. She cooked and sold food to people around in order to earn to provide for her daily needs. Just to be able to eat was enough for her together with a niece having a child. Before, she peddled to other towns with a group selling goods or items like *"patadjong,"* pillowcases, etc. This is known as *"pamolante"*. Finding it hard and tiring, she stopped and resorted to peddling around.

Maria was only seventeen when she left her place to spend a vacation at her uncle's place. Being young and pretty, she was eyed by a widower who also became her life partner. Before they lived together, Maria left for Mindanao to work; however, the man also followed her there. Automatically, they lived together in Mindanao. After three months, they were back at the man's place because Mindanao at that time was not peaceful because of the conflicts among the Muslims. Maria lived with him for almost thirty years without the benefit of marriage.

Later, they finally took their vows through what was called an *"emansabado"* or mass wedding officiated by a missionary in their place. The two lived together for almost 44 years but they were legally married for 14 years. Maria was happy living with him although they were childless and life was difficult because she had no stable job. Her husband was just a farmer with two children from his first wife.

In the 44 years of being with him, Maria was contented despite the hardships of life. Her husband got ill in his late 70s and Maria tried to take care of him in any way, especially through *"pamolante"*. When she was home, she would do laundry, cooking, and attend to his needs. It took one year for her husband to just stay physically helpless and experience pain and illness due to old age. However, when he felt an unusual pain in the stomach, she took him to the doctor for a checkup. He had a temporary alleviation but later on, he was found dead in the house. His death certificate showed that he died of appendicitis. Her husband's death brought Maria many tears, pain, self-pity, and insecurity.

Bereavement and Insecurity

Maria had just come from the market to buy their needs when she was informed that her husband died. At that time, he was in his house and taken care of by his daughter-in-law. Maria was staying in another house and she would just visit him every now and then. Maria shared that she was not welcomed in the family of her husband. She found herself in a difficult situation - being unaccepted in the family until he died. Maria hurriedly ran to the house crying, *Daw gintakluban ako ka langit*; (It seemed like the heaven had fallen apart), Maria said when she was asked of her initial reaction to the death of her husband. When she saw her husband lying lifeless, she hugged him tight. *Daw malumos ang dughan ko, nagpanaw tana wara gid ti ginhambal kun ano;* (My heart was drowned in deep sorrow. He did not say anything before it happened.)

The days that followed were full of sadness for Maria. She kept crying after seeing her husband in the coffin. She wailed as an expression of her grief, Bayaan mo run ako, kaluluoy lang ako; (You have left me, I am helpless), was what she shouted even during and after the burial. She said the pain was severe during the burial. She cried more knowing she could not see him anymore. Yet, she tried to control the tears because she was also concerned about her health.

For Maria and her husband, the couple's simple wish was to see another grandson in Maria's niece. Having no child of their own led her to wish for this, such that they would also enjoy the child's presence. Being able to eat was enough for her, and being together with her husband made her happy. She also shared she never had any regrets in life especially being with her husband for she did everything for him; she loved him so much.

Maria felt insecure when her husband died. She would often say *kaluluoy ako wara ako ti dangpan kapin pa wara ako ti pamilya.* (I feel insecure because there is no one to turn to. I don't have a family.)

When Maria became a widow, she experienced being teased by other people. Two men showed a fondness for her, yet she only ignored them. She believed they just wanted to tease her for being a widow at 65. When she was alone living with her niece having a child around, she stopped doing *"pamolante"*. She focused on selling food for herself and her niece. She carried on with that kind of job in

order to support her husband's needs while sick. Her income from selling was enough for their daily needs.

With the loss of her husband, Maria resorted to gambling. Influenced by other gamblers around, Maria played *"pangingue"* or playing cards in the neighborhood every afternoon. She found comfort in this vice after her husband passed away. Somehow, she had forgotten her sorrow about this pastime. She considered it a pastime since it helped her cope with her loneliness.

In the long years of being together, Maria had almost experienced a fulfilling life with her husband. Everything connected with her husband was important to her. At her age, she could not remember everything, especially the precious moments they had. She simply shared, *mga bayo na, makita, ko ginasinghut-singhotan ko;* (When I see his clothes, I kiss them.) Then, she would start sobbing. Occasions like "diez y nueve" reminded her of him. The occasion was somewhat connected with the event as she said. When she did tasks at home that would call for her husband's assistance, she would remember him, and she would start crying again.

Attending vigils for the dead in the neighborhood also reminded her of her husband, especially when he died just a year before. While being there made her tears flow for she recalled her loss, too. She would recall her last few moments with him. He seemed to be in need of attention and care.

According to Maria, she and her husband seldom fought even though they were childless. She also recalled that her husband told her that he would be sad leaving her alone.

Hearing the word *"balo"* (widow), she felt disgusted especially when somebody would tease courting her at that old age. She felt deeply saddened, thinking of the situation of being alone and helpless and having no one to be with in times of sorrow. She felt so insecure having no husband anymore. When asked what she has lost when her husband died, she said, *dura tanan, wara ka ti estoryahon, wara kaw ti pangayuan kun ano…. Budlay kabuhi ka balo, budlay gid, wara kaw ti gana magkaon;* (I lost all, there is no one to talk to, no one to give what you need; the life of a widow is hard, so difficult, there is no appetite to eat being alone.)

Getting Rid of Loneliness

Maria tried coping by drinking whiskey. She did it just to make her sleep better at night. She did not get drunk, she said. She consumed one bottle of whiskey for three days. She started drinking whiskey while her husband was in the state in the house during the wake. After the burial, she continued drinking. She would find means to buy liquor for, she said, it helped her a lot to have good sleep and to forget all her sadness. She joined talking with her nieces and sharing whatever in order to forget her depressive episodes. She visited other friends in the neighborhood to have people to talk to. If someone was dead in the neighborhood, she would join with others in the

vigil. She would stay longer in the vigil, *Una-una lang tana,* (He died ahead) was what she would say. This would give her relief, being with other widows.

As a food vendor, Maria spent most of her time cooking and enjoying her favorite drink as sleeping therapy.

The Day They Became Widows: A Reflection

When a husband dies, widows have a variety of emotional and behavioral responses and behaviors. Denying the death, anger, blame, and guilt, severe despair, appealing for more time and a second opportunity, and acceptance, recovery, and revival were all prevalent behavioral manifestations among widows.

Losing a husband means losing a companion, a life partner, and a confidante, as well as a sexual relationship and the other-self. It implies the loss of a wonderful provider and protector of the family. Losing a spouse is a traumatic loss that is akin to an "amputation" in the sense that a portion of the grieving individual is forever lost. Life appears to be meaningless.

Widows might progressively accept their loss and lessen the intensity of their anguish over time. A strong family solidarity offers an extremely helpful environment in which newly widowed persons can find strength and support during their grieving. Above all, a deep faith in God provides an emotionally fatigued or sad widow renewed hope and fortitude to face life.

ACKNOWLEDGMENT

My heartfelt gratitude to the following individuals for their unwavering support of these creative works:

Dr. Ma. Lulu L. Loyola (Mentor), Dr. Elnora V. Loriega, Dr. Grace E. Gomez, Dr. Hilda C. Montaño, Dr. Lee Y. Pineda, Prof. Timoteo O. Gasacao (Editor), Dr. Raul F. Muyong, Clarita T. Monteclaro, Sofia Espada-Bole, MFBC and NHFBC brethren, DCFeA, and the Dela Cruz Family. All honor and glory to God!

ABOUT THE AUTHOR

SHIRLEY D. FRIGILLANO is Associate Professor V of Iloilo Science and Technology University Miagao Campus. She finished her Master of Arts in English, major in Linguistics, and Doctor of Philosophy in Education, major in Psychology and Guidance in Education, at West Visayas State University, Iloilo City. She pursued and finished her Doctor of Education in English Language Teaching at Cebu Normal University, Cebu City as a Commission on Higher Education (CHED) Scholar.

She is a researcher, an accreditor, and an internal ISO auditor. She is married to William P. Frigillano, a seafarer. She has two sons, Eros Gwen and Mishael Shem. She is one of the BODs of Doane Christian Fellowship Academy, Inc., Miagao, Iloilo.